the One Sea

Voices from the Deep

Acknowledgements and thanks to:

My fellow voyagers on our epic journey through Ramsey Sound by kayak, summer 2006, when the idea for 'the One Sea' was born . . . and to the porpoises of Pembrokeshire.

Bill and Georgia Sinclair - editing and concept development

An early inspiration was Jacques Cousteau and the 'Calypso'. In his 1975 TV series 'The Ocean World of Jacques Cousteau', he said "on the ocean, man is a hunter only. He takes but returns little."

Images: Lucy Siveter of imagequestmarine.com

National Oceanic and Atmospheric Administration - www.noaa.gov

Cover photograph:

Spinner dolphins by
Masa Ushioda/
imagequestmarine.com

Next Generation Preschool
2508 Galen Dr.
Champaign, IL 61821

the One Sea

Voices from the Deep

David Pierce Hughes

They are men of the Sea, my boys,
there's not a wave goes by I don't think of them.

The One Sea - Voices from the Deep

First published in Great Britain in 2007

ISBN 978-1-905470-20-4   1-905470-20-7
British Library CIP Data
A catalogue record of this book is available from the British Library

www.seasquirt.net

Published by SeaSquirt Books
Ty Ganol   Rhodiad y Brenin   St Davids Pembrokeshire   Wales

Concept and design by David Hughes and Jane Messore

Printed and bound by Gomer Press Limited, Wales

the One Sea
Voices from the Deep

About the paper on which
The One Sea book is printed.

¶ Paper is made from fibres that are found in the cell walls of all plants. The fibres mainly come from plant sources such as wood, bamboo, cotton, jute, or even rice. However wood from trees is the main source of fibres used in paper making. A mixture of water and fibres is filtered through a screen to make a sheet of paper. When the paper is dried chemical bonds form to give the paper its strength.

The One Sea book is printed on paper in which at least 75% of the fibre has been recycled. This means it comes from materials that have been used before.

The main types of papers from which recycled paper is made are:
- Newspapers, magazines, directories and leaflets.
- Office and computer used paper
- Carboard from boxes and packaging
- Mixed or coloured papers

 NAPM approved
recycled product

This book is printed on Revive Matt from the Robert Horne Group, which contains at least 75% de-inked post-consumer waste fibre.

ontents

Inside the Magic Cave . . .

In Xanadu did the relentless wave
where Gaia the sacred river ran
through labyrinths only seen by man
down to the magic cave.

Listen now and you will hear
the One Sea's message for the human ear.

Long after travelling miles and miles
the wave does flow with cunning wiles,
arriving in the magic cave, when found,
it's walls all rough, grey, black and brown
with shells and seaweed covering all the ground.

And in that strange and darkened place
messages can be read upon the wall,
as if by a strange force displayed,
always and only delivered by the wave.

These messages come from the deep
where turtles, algae, whales and sharks do speak.
And now we humans need to listen hard
to messages coming from near and far.
For in this book what you will find
is what you already know within your mind.

. . . the Wave delivers
a message for
the human race

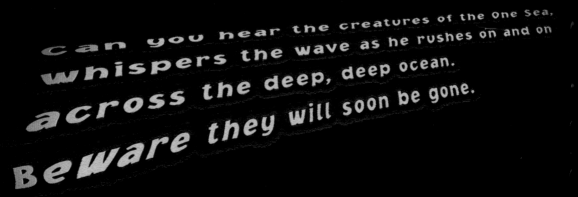

Can you hear the creatures of the One Sea,
whispers the wave as he rushes on and on
across the deep, deep ocean.
Beware they will soon be gone.

We must awake from our selfish slumber.
The Sea, the deep, are not ours to plunder.
We must stand back from mad pollution
so Sea and Man find the solution.

We must treat the Oceans as a garden,
where plants will grow when left to ripen.

So listen now to these creatures from the deep.
The oceans of the Earth are not ours to wreck.
These messages must wake us from our sleep,
for if we don't awake, we all shall weep.

Ask yourself the vital question.
What are we doing, you and me,
to the glorious, deep mysterious One Sea?

11

We have roamed the deep, deep ocean,
forty million years or more.
Gently sailing on our chosen routes
over ten thousand miles of ocean roar.

We feed on krill and plankton,
and sing our songs from sea to shore;
we listen across thousands of miles
to hear the one that we adore.

The Whale

You, Man, you harpoon us,
and kill us without shame.
Now you poison our waters;
it's your waste that is to blame.

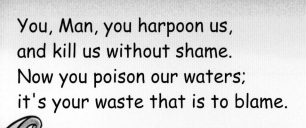Can you hear the Humpback Whale?
whispers the Wave as it rushes on and on,
across the deep, deep ocean,
endangered by the Tribe of Man.

The
Polar
Bear

The whitest white is the place we live,
where we wander on our way;
but now it's getting warmer
as more icebergs melt each day.

We travel farther and farther
when hunting for food and fish.
It's harder to feed our families,
so our numbers are getting less.

The ice floes break up sooner,
and our hunting season grows shorter.
So many of us go hungry,
and we have less time for son or daughter.

Can you hear the noble Polar Bear?
whispers the Wave as it rushes on and on,
across the deep, deep ocean.
Beware, they will soon be gone.

15

The Albatross

Flying day and night across the sky
we ride the trade winds, soaring high;
and glide for days and days on end,
to hunt the slippery Squid.

Our enemy is the fish hooks
that trail behind your boats,
which we mistake for fish
and get caught in your floats.

In a lifetime of mighty travel,
we can fly over three million miles;
so why become our enemy,
and put us through these trials?

Can you hear the cry of the Albatross?
whispers the Wave as it rushes on and on,
across the deep, deep ocean,
betrayed by the Tribe of Man.

The Turtle

We roam the seven oceans,
and swim from sea to land;
we survive the harshest storms
to lay our eggs upon the sand.

Our newborn start their journey
and waddle to the sea,
they swim out in the ocean
to where they think they're free.

But then they meet the nets
that you drag across the waves,
and get tangled in great numbers
and sink to their watery graves.

Can you hear the loveable Turtle?
whispers the Wave as it rushes on and on,
across the deep, deep ocean.
Beware, they will soon be gone.

The Lobster

The Crab

We are the crustaceous Crab.
We patrol the ocean floors
with our ten legs, walking sideways;
but then you grab our claws.

You rip us from our crabitat.
You take a million tonnes each year.
Which is why we tell our young ones
that they must live in fear.

We are the obstinate Lobster,
we swim backward quite a lot;
but then you boil up water,
and chuck us in the pot.

Can you hear the tough Crustaceans?
whispers the Wave as it rushes on and on,
across the deep, deep ocean
with a message meant for Man.

The Sea Urchin

The Starfish

22

A lurchin' Urchin wanders by
and stops to chat and say:
Pollution is our enemy,
it just will not go away.

And though we are really spiky,
you catch us when you can;
you even like to eat us,
especially in Japan.

Our cousins are the Starfish.
They sail round and round,
but your oil slicks defeat them
when they wash up on the ground.

Can you hear the Spiky Urchin?
whispers the Wave as it rushes on and on,
across the deep, deep ocean
to the cave where Man has gone.

The Wave wonders . . .

Can you hear the creatures of the sea?
shouts the Wave as it rages on and on
across the deep, deep blue ocean
to the Cave where Man has gone.

Are you listening, Man? demands the Wave
as it rushes on its way.
Why do you mistreat the One Sea
each night and every day.

And now the Wave grows taller
as it rushes on and on
over the deep, deep ocean.
Beware! Where has the great Wave gone?

Algae and Plankton

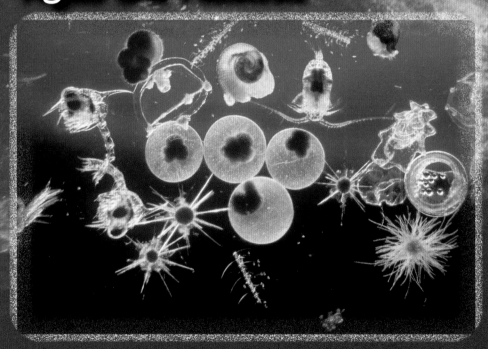

We are the extraordinary Algae.
Through sunlight and water and CO_2
we make our own food and oxygen,
and gather on top of the deep, deep blue.

We Plankton drift the currents
to spread out on the salty sea,
providing tons of food for fishes,
fellow creatures, you and me.

We are the food source of the ocean,
an important member of the band,
yet we're threatened by your boats,
and pollution from the land.

Can you hear the Plankton and Algae?
whispers the Wave as it rushes on and on,
across the deep, deep ocean
with a message meant for Man.

The Great Coral Reef

Why is the water warming?
asks the great, great Coral reef
that grows from skeletons forming,
with colour beyond belief.

So Coral makes a garden,
a garden in the sea,
where fish and plants and creatures
can grow and thrive and be.

But now your diving disturbs us,
and breaks our delicate branches;
and warmer water destroys us,
and your oil spills spoil our dances.

Can you hear the glorious Coral?
whispers the Wave as it rushes on and on,
across the deep, deep ocean.
Beware, it will soon be gone.

The Squid

The Octopus

We Squid can change our colour,
or spray you with our ink.
We can move around quite slowly
or fast as you can blink.

Some of us are small,
others grow to giant size;
over twenty metres tall,
to stare right in your eyes.

Our Octopus cousins have eight arms,
and jet their way along.
We both have true blue blood,
so don't you treat us wrong.

Can you hear the slippery Squid?
whispers the Wave as it rushes on and on,
across the deep, deep ocean,
with a message meant for Man.

The Shark

We are the streamlined Shark,
famous for our powerful jaws.
We hunt the Squid in light and dark,
as we obey nature's laws.

We move with amazing speed,
like jet-powered ocean machines.
We are attracted by scent and blood,
and often haunt your dreams.

Each year a million Sharks must die,
pursued by boats, alone or in groups.
You catch us and throw our bodies away,
keeping our fins to flavour your soups.

Can you hear the streamlined Shark?
whispers the Wave as it rushes on and on,
across the deep, deep ocean,
with a message meant for Man.

33

The Dolphin

We swim, we hunt, we cruise,
in seas both calm and rough;
we leap out from the ocean,
then dive for all we're worth.

We love you, Dolphins hear Man say,
like friends from long ago;
but how can Dolphins truly know
when Man is friend or foe?

You say we are so clever,
you think we go to school;
but our future really is in doubt,
for it's Man who plays the fool.

Can you hear the trusting Dolphin?
whispers the Wave as it rushes on and on,
across the deep, deep ocean.
Beware, they will soon be gone.

The Penguin

Have you seen the Penguin shuffle?
Have you seen the Penguin flap?
Have you seen the Penguin underwater
like a torpedo glides from its trap?

Have you met the mighty Emperor,
the bravest Penguin of them all,
warming the hatchling for sixty-five days,
in the harshest conditions of all.

We live in the coldest Antarctic,
on our feet we raise our chicks;
till they hatch and slide to the ocean,
to take their first swimming kicks.

Can you hear the voice of the Penguin?
whispers the Wave as it rushes on and on,
down to the wall of the Magic Cave,
with a message meant for Man.

The Abyss

The Worm

The Anglerfish

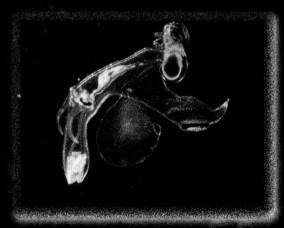

The Heteropod Snail

Deep down in the twilight zone,
where Man hardly ever goes,
lives the heteropod transparent Snail, alone,
with his teeth on the end of his nose.

Stranger than strange, deep in the Abyss,
live creatures that glow in the dark;
and enormous Worms and Anglerfish,
who hunt as they give off a spark.

Here in the deepest darkest home,
we creatures are less troubled by Man.
That's good for us, so leave us alone
to live out our lives as we can.

Can you hear voices from the deepest Deep?
whispers the Wave as it rushes on and on,
down and into the Magic Cave,
with the darkest message for Man.

. . . the Wave delivers
a warning message for
the human race

Can you hear the creatures of the One Sea,
whispers the wave as he rushes on and on
across the deep, deep ocean.
Beware they will soon be gone.

At last the Wave begins to wonder,
has Man heard those messages
from creatures living under
the deep, blue One Sea?

"You are not listening, Man,
the Wave begins to shout.
You still pollute and plunder
as though you have the right
to steal from the ocean
each day and every night."

And now, beneath the setting sun
the Wave grows higher and higher
as though roused by a great and terrible anger,
stirred by the wind like a roaring fire.

The Wave repeats: Beware, beware,
now is the time to show you care.

So listen again, for we all must hear
the One Sea's message for the human ear

Masa Ushioda/imagequestmarine.com

NOAA Photo Library - Harley D. Nygren

Fritz Poelking/V&W/imagequestmarine.com

Scott Tuason/imagequestmarine.com

Michael Nolan/V&W/imagequestmarine

James D Watt/imagequestmarine.com

Michael Nolan/V&W/imagequestmarine.com

Masa Ushioda/imagequestmarine.com

Klaus Jost/imagequestmarine.com

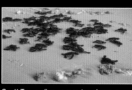

Scott Tuason/imagequestmarine.com

Masa Ushioda/imagequestmarine.com

James D Watt/imagequestmarine.com

OAR/National Undersea Research Program

James D Watt/imagequestmarine.com

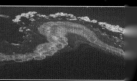

Roger Steene/imagequestmarine.com

James D Watt/imagequestmarine.com

Dr. James P. McVey, NOAA Program

PHOTO CREDITS

PHOTO CREDITS

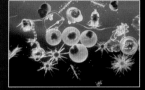

Peter Parks/imagequestmarine.com

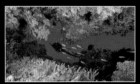

James D Watt/imagequestmarine.com

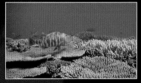

Ove Hoegh-Guldberg Centre for Marine
Studies University of Queensland

James D Watt/iPeter Parks/ magequestmarine

NOAA Photo Library

James D Watt/imagequestmarine.com

Klaus Jost/imagequestmarine.com

Masa Ushioda/imagequestmarine.com

Kike Calvo/V&W/imagequestmarine.com

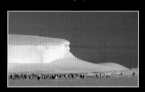

Fritz Poelking/V&W/imagequestmarine.com

SOC/imagequestmarine.com

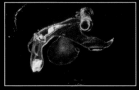

Peter Parks/imagequestmarine.com

Peter Batson/imagequestmarine.com

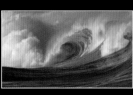

James D Watt/imagequestmarine.com

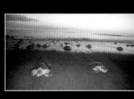

Scott Tuason/imagequestmarine.com

James D Watt/imagequestmarine.com

Florida Keys National Marine Sanctuary